THE
VAULT

ANDRÉS
CERPA

ALICE JAMES BOOKS
Farmington, ME
alicejamesbooks.org

10 9 8 7 6 5 4 3 2 1

Alice James Books are published by Alice James Poetry Cooperative, Inc., an affiliate of
the University of Maine at Farmington.

Alice James Books
114 Prescott Street
Farmington, ME 04938
www.alicejamesbooks.org

Library of Congress Cataloging-in-Publication Data

Names: Cerpa, Andrés, 1990– author.
Title: The vault / Andrés Cerpa.
Description: Farmington. ME : Alice James Books, 2021
Identifiers: LCCN 2020045536 (print) | LCCN 2020045537 (ebook)
   ISBN 9781948579186 (trade paperback) | ISBN 9781948579421 (epub)
Subjects: LCGFT: Poetry.
Classification: LCC PS3603.E747 V38 2021 (print) | LCC PS3603.E747 (ebook)
   DDC 811/.6—dc23
LC record available at https://lccn.loc.gov/2020045536
LC ebook record available at https://lccn.loc.gov/2020045537

Alice James Books gratefully acknowledges support from individual donors, private
foundations, the University of Maine at Farmington, the National Endowment for
the Arts, the Amazon Literary Partnership, and the Maine Arts Commission, an
independent state agency supported by the National Endowment for the Arts.

Cover art photo provided by Andrés Cerpa
Interior photos by and Henry & Co. and Lukas Robertson

I

JOIN
ME

my proclivity toward ruin has only increased with my distance from it

listening to *Born to Be Blue* at a friend's place in Walton NY

burning one down

I became so used to the unrequited life

the one more for the ruin

the hurricane stars

that I strain to sing love in love

the inexplicable whole

    the it without antecedent

    the fog that forms like a father disintegrating in a purple chair

who am I without my clothes & friends

    my linens

snow on the ocean unseen

    on the coldest day of this November

we made a day of it

    it

laid there for hours as our mice crept into the stove

despair & I are inventing a word

      world by world

marked by a long lifeline & a canyon of darkness what I want to uncover

      & bury at once

today I woke next to Julia after a simple & resonant night

      slowly

we are saying things

      leave a toothbrush   see me on your bad days too

the winter before her

      I staid home smoked & toasted the night

the stars must be lonely

      the word is

somewhere in summer fireflies shaken to life in a jar

dear Gregorio

maybe I can inspire you to hate yourself more

    because the days have become me & your story

that sad thing you left

    now Uncle Robert takes Dad by the shoulders & jokes

do you see me

    they impersonate you

& are not

    but let's get right down to the subject

the drinking

    the creation of distance

the more

    I see you

you enter the city & the whole monstrosity shivers

there is a silence in the seam with which to break pills

  a chainsaw outside making damn sure an unknown fire

doesn't reach the house

  coyote howl & tranquil cougar

my .34 caliber heart

  steeped in the river

buried out back

  my almost bloom

I wish I could feel the particulars

  more particulars

  how Julia asked me to stop repeating my fear that she'll leave me

so often like you're trying to plant that seed

dear Gregorio

how long you've been dead is etched like an island

it grows the way trackers on whales fall apart

I thought I saw you the way Dad did at 7

on a corner asleep

we both turned away

can you hear every muffled thing & none of what's spoken

will I drown in a water I won't drink

the flock moves through the sky like ruin & I am only the man I am today

    come winter

the branches will net the 4 p.m. twilight & the absence of birds

    I am all of this season within season

on my third beer

    unhinged dream as my sinew

ready to lay down until the snow leans the branches to net me in quiet

    a fawn emerges after the after

its muzzle buried in snow

    it is now the after

the gray sky so close & impossible

    to exhume

dear Gregorio

my eyes close & a gun meant for me sounds

    like some sort of redemption

it's easy to imagine a hell

    but a heaven

you left this world as if there were others

    in a paced & lucid manner

it happened

    it happens in fractions & cirrhosis light

in silence

    I hold Julia

like the hours that remain & breathe covertly as we kiss

carelessness & fear & not wanting the intensity of the moment

    where I give myself over & possibly cry

the move from gunpowder branches post-rain to enclosure

I've hurt for such little comfort

    like a bird's first test of the glass

dear Julia

what it means to me to become a man is to hold you in the place I rent

& know there's a world

it seems so simple

to say fuck being bound by my wolfskin coat & mean it

dear Colin

we do so much to hurt ourselves

when we left the Blue & Gold with the simple turn

of your back & mine away from each other

the city took over

I could not hear your voice & soon its body

a succession of so many lives we do not see

birds at midnight two rivers

chaos blurred & seamed

this dilated language somehow got connected to all that we do

but truly what do I know about my own life

& why now

more light

more fucking light

remember

how since Homer

since fire

everything old in everything flocks to another sunlit tree

it only recently became spring & already the shattered glass that lines this

by-the-water road

    where only teenagers & addicts & fishermen drink

has disappeared

    it's a damn good place to die

    Carl did

where the thigh-high weeds gut fish in the wind

    & laughter rises like blood through the texture of a sock

the trail is sun-dyed overgrown & old

    it is the rot we attempt to dispel

    strengthened by oil

& the black sand of a thousand chemistry sets

    but everything comes back

alive & in the process of mystery

    another heron dives below the water to eat

the beer in my jacket is warm & amounts to comfort

as I welcome the winter of my 26th year

& the world as it must goes still

the days slip by in a slime of grief

the way in Amsterdam

three days into a bender

I sat like two wolves transparent in hunger

I don't want another drink

the quartz breeze in my coat as I lifted my collar

I want the past like a harvest again

dear Gregorio

the whole city is dog shit & late nights

glassware in damp boxes

so I turn towards things that are far

to die or to die will come back in its innocent way

in a fuck-you foxhole moment

a script & a rolled-up hundred like taking my palm to the breaker

at the museum on Sunday

sudden owls

pinhole camera glacier & hawk

on the station platform a snap of wind followed by my reflection

      those riders riding through me

as if I were a ghost or had wings

      & their reflections on the opposite Plexiglas pane

which is both tunnel-wall & mirror

      I have seen them in restaurant windows as I pass alone

rooftop

      palm of light

in my one life

      I have stood above the labyrinth

& touched what is not there

dear Gregorio

is dead the same piss-stained mattress you didn't feel then

or do you wake to the coils as they char now

often

I took your son into my arms

as he choked

even on air

I'd like to give you a shave & see that we don't look alike

that you were mostly rubble

it must have felt like the years

watching your father

the noose

eclipse of my life

love of my sight

have we stained the same snow

dear Julia

I've buried generations of trees without reason

immense in their grandness

they grow in my chest & are ruthless for light

dear Julia

I try not to cry in your presence

but sometimes I wake from sleep already in tears

I've never moved to hold you then

but sometimes

in the morning

while we wake

I reach out with such joy it seems that the singing that has carried the world

from darkness into the torch

of our life is right here in our hands

the veins & the lungs & the lost fountains that relieve every thirst

just for a moment

there is no brine to clench my skin no well

I feel old

like I've only been alive today

I could go on & on about regret but what I retain is not frivolous

    compile my youth

letters

    the excitement of new drugs

birthmark & the way she slipped through a fence off the highway

    the horizon

a fortress abandoned except for her eyes

failure I say

      as the starlings dart in the last feed before the heavy machinery turns

      the water to dusk

then Mike falls uncharacteristically silent

I was the best man at his wedding

      & now our lives move in two different directions yet in tandem

that's my friend as I liquor up & backflip into the pool

that's my friend as he opens the door to his first house

at every stage in our life we've said *it's a strange stage in our life*

embers more vivid at dusk

      soon we'll get into the car

& I'll go home to an empty apartment

      have another as I run my hands through the few strands left

on the second pillow

      I am haunted by names

chain smokers forgetting to drag as a thousand black birds move

through the street like a frost

a certain beauty

in *that'll never happen again*

after 26 years in New York a few months abroad & a summer upstate

what did I learn

the forces of nature although merciless accept natural decay the ocean is yours now

    & clay

& the goose bumps across my body & the youth of my back

    you

without knowing

    claimed so much of this world forever

in the span of a day

dear burial

what in my life has a membrane

what cannot quite be touched

I want it all to be true

      what I say to her

yet they ether

      the dancers

      the wings

always sometimes sometimes in fog

      gondola

but really a leather jacket left in a cab gone cold

      there are calendars

cross streets

      postcards

& calls

      wanting to be alone

then not

      then wanting it back

Venice in July together *Venice in July* alone

when I put my arm around her

     looked back

five or so mice emerged from the ground

     automated disgust

kill

     mindlessness & poison

my arm around her

     the park in her elegant hands

small bites & bread

     she told me to feed them

     feed them

the phone falls through my hands & I am left with salt water

    whalebone in history

wolf in the stars

    then all the skeletal keys not yet written & all at once

blood-let in the chamber of night

    methodically cleaning my apartment

doing lines alone

I have tamped down the earth & prayed for the vault to open

    neglect

all my psychological shit untouched

when I imagine myself

    I am always leaving

I couldn't draw my own face if god asked

when I think of the intricate design

    glaciers cutting up mountains & how my interior system

    seems contrary to the world

park benches with a bump in the middle so the homeless can't sleep

    abandoned stars

in August

    I planned to overdose into the ocean in a foreign city

at the end of the week

    there are only so many versions of not there

all of me & the future of me & the sad possibilities that aren't ourselves

we met on the cliffs

    birthmark the size of a sparrow on her abs that she asked me to kiss

in return

    I would've been nothing else if given the choice like a gift

dear Julia

like a bundle of filthy stars I am wrought to the heath by a wolf in the absence

of language

forgive me

I've come to your door as a stranger

excuse after vivid excuse

the last subtle keys in the last moments of the last song

milk hitting the coffee

the embers so red & cedar in the fiber of my wolfskin coat

I've got more than enough time to not live

who would'a thunk it

all the times I wanted to cry & couldn't

all the times I was about to & stopped

dear Gregorio

there was a sadness I once let a woman touch

but like you

the moment is over

it lingers

you linger in double exposure & blood

please

rise from the vault & say *yes*

I see you

most if not all of what you hold

dear Julia

I want to write love & completion not affair or a future self or the blood-

speckled horses of war

grandeur

looms in the dense oceans we slip easily through

salt

the heart joins the water like snow

& one day I'll lift the collar of my wolf & walk away

I can feel it

the transient nature

the snow that hangs in my heart like a thoroughbred noose

just the sun going down is enough to obliterate everything I love

I experience the world in dramatic fractions

in the vows of our bodies & tongue

we drove up in the dark & missed two exits as we spoke

then bluestone magnesium flint

needles & brush

& the nest you lifted

to kneel beside & grow

by morning

we realized the leaves had turned in full

my lies & faux freedom hidden like that

if only the day

& when you said *deep in thought*

I murmured *the ocean*

for so long

your hands the river

benevolent weir

I'm still here I still murder a few nights a week but treat the morning well

    coffee slow waking a book

fear of my unknown

    dust & its gentle shatter

stunted opportunity after stunted opportunity

    a text that reads *en route*

Let there be a vault

*to divide the waters of heaven
from the waters of the earth.*

II

THE
NIGHTMARE
TOUCHED
ITS
FOREHEAD
TO
MY
LIPS

Who will say a few words now that the tomb is gone?

Thunder in our sleep. The wrong way back

to begin. Animal need for affection.

Anvil,

or like two rooms that never touch,

I arrive.

The nightmare touched its forehead to my lips.

::

Then a year where I wouldn't let him enter —

not this book or the book of the dead.

::

Four plates set at the table.

::

The noose in my chest

tenses at *we*.

::

Half the ashes in a Ziploc in the dresser.

Half the ashes in the crypt.

::

The nightmare touched its forehead to my lips.

It must be pressed against your body in sleep.

Encapsulated. The cold shaking like a lover.

Unenterable pixels — miles
 like years away.

                ::

Dream — *I worried my tears would ruin her shirt.*

                ::

Taught to listen by three chairs, or the ocean
remained on my tongue.

                ::

Deep in the formless. Somewhere I've never been,

a figure kneels

            & I kneel with it.

        ::

The vault I'm trying to enter
tastes like ocean

 & hides another sky.

The sky feels like a K-pin
doused with some other shit that'll kill you —
        infectious harp.

        ::

The space between language —
shard of porcelain
        from the dictator's house.

        ::

Looking back —
so many lives like veils undressed
        in the sullen dark.

        ::

Names etched on my heart.

        ::

Be grateful, the whole future isn't a skull —
blue silk in the gray matter
        like water from sand.

Dear lord,

I pronounce your name & believe
I don't believe.

Why'd you kill my father
through 17 years,

then let him kill himself?

    ::

A system of migratory birds
in a bamboo forest.

I can hear them
though they're hidden.

I can hear them
like closing all of my eyes.

The bird was ripped of its wings by another

just like it. Careful. This could be you.

Both birds in a necklace. I surrender,

if only to quell the questions from the ground.

The ground, filled with little bird bones & apples.

Cool to the touch. I surrender. Brutal

laughter goes the psalm.

Look away. Leave the hounds in their cages.

::

The tool of distance let me survive.

::

Cocaine summer. Affair. TV.

::

The first year I woke to him drowning.

::

I slept in his hair.

::

That's my pop, I repeated.

::

More Dilaudid. DNR.

::

Maybe he'll outlast the night.

::

Draino is a base & not an acid.

::

Red —

so much red as he drowned.

Dear Mom,

We grieve on

different time lines.

Alley of green

gunmetal ocean.

I have yet to visit

the crypt.

It's not addiction if you're doing it right.

If the world goes unnoticed
& you're the only one there.

        ::

Nothing new
can save me

from grief. Even the morning
is a blue remnant

cut with a razor —

the residue I lick from the book.

I meant what I said in the letters —

I am weaker than you imagine & less honest.

When I lay still enough,

I feel like I can hold it, or it holds me. Something's changed.

I stepped into the staircase with the sound of silk

& the smell of sleeping dogs. The secret — in three seamless moments,

the kind of life one doesn't forget.

In time we'll be so outside time that we'll laugh.
Though holding your hand, etc.

      ::

The coffee's almost done
& the good advice won't stand up
to the chemical catharsis.

      ::

Snow day with codeine.
Gray in your hair. Still life
in a life unfinished.

      ::

Without a road, even the silence
touched its lungs to the ground.

Find me, or carry the dark threshold three years away.

     ::

Did I ever tell you the story, how a gang of us rode deep into the country

then walked our bikes to the burnt façade. Arranged in the wheat,

doors & windows. A gallery where the deer slipped away.

     ::

Snow today & my breath meets the dial-tone sky.

Where to scatter the second half of your ashes

when anywhere outside the poem, I've yet to say *dead*?

Linen curtain with a pattern like rain,
let me sleep another hour

though the bed is a piss stain
& the morning's now gone.

    ::

Beyond? or *Find another prayer.*

    ::

Ancient sun, all fire & brimstone,
let me be the hidden,
the sparrow I once caressed.

Bit by bit I'll go on surviving.

Love like the sheets tumbled soft.

Miles of snow outside Lisbon. Before turning the camera

to the window, *Soon, I'll let you go.*

They say that love continues.

That the ghosts or angels will usher us home.

February again & the table begs for fruit.

And what do you want to be told?

That a bottle of pills will do

as well as a car for escape? a ticket toward?

Lace & black denim in the blur.

Years later, I woke like bluestone from the sea.

A radiant silence

envelopes my veins

with its letter —

Dad,

I still need you.

Little wave
in thought.

Blank architecture
that holds me.

This is a little psalm
in the moon-

struck snow.
Thank you,

for I haven't been
patient as promised.

Thank you,
for the desperate

Hopper-esque light.

*There is so little
to hold*, I said

as I held it. Each
bloom

of strength
that entered

my hands.

The stars must be doped out the way they flicker
& refuse to answer my calls.

I prefer waking,
but frail hours, cold sleep. Enough time

then never enough.

Overdose —

I'd like to put the night in a cage
& let it breed like two finches.

All the eggs that won't hatch but mothered.

The antlers merge into every hidden thing
beneath a purple & growing sky
as Colin broadens his shoulders.
We will not pass the bridge. Tracks
soften. Cells go dead.
My shoes like a stagnant river. *I am cold,*
Joe says, as he loosens his hair from his hood. Spiders waking
to prey on the clouds. My backpack waits
like a bed. *Remember when is the lowest form of conversation,*
so we let its warmth breed in the hourglass snow.
Colin crosses the river by stones.
Ice in its arteries dance toward a harp. On the way back,
blankets thrown over our shoulders. *Forgive me,*
I say. Beyond this steel wool is another threshold.
Its deathbed purple is alive & well.

Place does not solve this —
room with better light
or more trees.

Ordinary acts.

                    ::

I own no land & my dog's long gone.

                    ::

There are journeys we never return from —

Honduras at 19.
The poem.
Heroin.
March 5th.

I keep learning the same lessons.

::

Obliterate & sun drenched & just a little bit longer.

Not numb,

but what I'll remember,

as the last snow falls through the ceiling,

falls through the bed.

::

Quiet love,

god's been stomping the ether with the physical world

to sell it for cheap. And I'm buying

my way with my little addict heart.

::

Threadbare fruit flies pattern in the kitchen like splendor,

so we wake to splendor.

The blueprint — love is loyal & sudden. It grows

the way a hand reaches out to a growl.

But now that migration moves through me

like passing clouds hinged to the underbelly fur,

I watch myself

as we huddle in bed. In each vastness,

death sets fire to the sea.

For the living, water. And now,

you're all the wells mined for their depth.

All of the silence

& all of the *all*s I can conjure.

You are not in the living room.

You are not in your chair.

I drove to the end of the world today.

Snow in the forecast,

so I left my bicycle

& the other half of your ashes at home.

Flame in my clothes

like a hangover that courses the folds

for years. Every trace of horizon

now gone. In a foreign car, painted in snow salt,

I watch myself drift out.

Then low tide where I walk ankle-deep,

careful not to cut up my feet.

A bit of flame in the wind. Blood

in the flash. There is no god,

so I move my own heaven.

Pull back the chaos like a dancing star or a blanket.

::

No gift but the absence followed by song.

::

Twilit map with no river,

though there's a river in earshot

like a dream of home.

::

Together we tested the water.

::

Now, saudade

as you explained it —

::

Here I am lord,

so far from your ocean.

::

Confession — the shard of porcelain

rings in every room.

The jaws open & I see my own face. Likeness of my father,
strange archetypal ground for a tongue —

::

Power of falls & pine.

::

In a tundra I never asked for
& forgave —

purple chair where he sat.

::

How many years will I open
& not find him?

::

The yellow at the base of the molars
becomes the whole sky.

I read the wind too soon —

Orphic brail of ocean,

27 stones in the yard.

The pills are waiting to connect the image —

17 birds & a love song

that passed. Too often,

I believe them. Late, I walk through town,

a blanket over my shoulders,

& leave each question

a note — *The pills are waiting*

to dissolve the day

into a bearable likeness.

The pills are waiting to dissolve the day.

At the end of the world, the sign reads,

We'll see you next summer.

When will the vault descend?

When will the code emerge

from the ocean? Take me,

dear lord, if you're out there,

to the end of the end

of us, where the whales breathe the threshold

& the seeds run fallow at best.

I grieve anew.

In untethered sleep, the season

buries the hidden.

Whatever it is I'll miss will return

like a stranger. What I wanted.

What I always had.

   ::

Notebook — *I've been sleeping late. Well into the afternoon or longer,*

  waiting for darkness to open my eyes.

To remove my own heaven,

I walk. Snarl the field.

Hitch my boat & lie down.

It's a simple plan,

be simple. Make tea.

Wake up & breath a bit before the future.

It's a long walk home

walking backwards.

I've yet to give my oar to the sea.

Mire of silence. Raven of days. Forgiven,

but not for the living.

Forgiven, like unearthing the bulbs.

I could only hope to be hopeless.

That my cell phone would die

& all of this silence could have

a location.

A black square. A name.

I thought that when my father died I'd get something back.

Thank you. The vague momentum

swirls in an afterlife I cannot measure.

The room walked away

the way a wolf gets its sea legs

in a shipping container.

Everything not had

then had,

& more often. The prescription pad

did a dance. In the alley —

womb-like, summer's

5 a.m. blue. Within the cage

of each willow, the distance

sounds like music.

There is always somewhere

to hide.

Dear Dad,

You are nowhere I've ever been

rebuilt. Kitchen table, purple chair,

the whorl of your ring on my chest.

I place his ring in the ashtray

before Julia arrives.

Nowhere compiles with precision

like dust into books.

Birthday card. Voice mail.

If the ring were to flare

with her body, both ocean & river,

I'd drown.

The flock sparks & we turn toward each other for meaning.

::

Wolf I never saw. Trees I'll never enter. Tide pools that must be the end.

::

The ways in which we yearn to be nurtured.

::

Notebook — *My vigor against time has drained. How to meet the day?*

::

Whales up north breaking the surface.

::

Fever of dream.

::

The options — reinvent my loss or fail to recover.

The real goes unanswered —

god, afterlife,

migration. And when I asked in the first dream

why he hadn't come sooner —

You have to travel first to return.

Beyond the poem —
with Julia,
always.

NOTES

"More light more fucking light" is a line by Colin Schmidt.

"The vows of our body & tongue" is a variation of a line from James Baldwin's *Tell Me How Long the Train's Been Gone.*

A misremembered translation of Genesis 1:6 holds each sequence.

"Snow day with codeine" is the title of a Graham Foust poem.

"Remember when is the lowest form of conversation" is taken from Episode 80 of the HBO series *The Sopranos.*

"Dancing star" is a phrase from Fredrick Nietzsche.

ACKNOWLEDGMENTS

Thank you to the editors, readers, & journal staff that published sections of this book: *The Academy of American Poets, The Nation, Ploughshares, Frontier Poetry, Foundry Journal, On the Seawall, Horsethief, The Rumpus, The Offing, & Solstice: A Magazine of Diverse Voices.*

Eternal gratitude to Alice James Books.

RECENT TITLES FROM ALICE JAMES BOOKS

ALICE JAMES BOOKS is committed to publishing books that matter. The press was founded in 1973 in Boston, Massachusetts as a cooperative, wherein authors performed the day-to-day undertakings of the press. This element remains present today, as authors who publish with the press are invited to collaborate closely in the publication process of their work. AJB remains committed to its founders' original feminist mission, while expanding upon the scope to include all voices and poets who might otherwise go unheard. In keeping with its efforts to build equity and increase inclusivity in publishing and the literary arts, AJB seeks out poets whose writing possesses the range, depth, and ability to cultivate empathy in our world and to dynamically push against silence. The press was named for Alice James, sister to William and Henry, whose extraordinary gift for writing went unrecognized during her lifetime.

Designed by Alban Fischer

Printed by McNaughton & Gunn

3/22